Bichon Frise

Unique Among Dogs

By John Williams

Contents

Congratulations! You won't find a better companion than you're little sturdy Bichon Frise. Unique among dogs, he's especially made to be your companion and makes a good friend. He's a unique and beautiful dog, whether as a pet or in the ring. Either way, I know you'll be pleased. Not large at all, the Bichon Frise weighs in at approximately 5 to 10 kg (10 to 20 lbs.) and stands at 20 to 30 cm (9 to 12 in.) Sometimes they can be slightly larger.

When prepared for show, you'll want him clipped to show off his body in a compact round appearance. The tail, carried over the back, will be long and curly. His ears will be drop-covered in cropped long hair.

Description

The double-layered coat is silky soft. The outer coat is 3 – 4 inches (7 to 10 cm) long, coarse and curly: the undercoat is soft and dense. This is what gives this dog its powder-puff unique quality. You won't have to worry about allergies either. Some are less curly than others. Their fur ranges in color from solid white, cream, grey and apricot. White is the preferred show color if you're thinking of showing off your little pride and joy. A small tint of buff, cream or apricot color sometimes shows up around the ears, snout, paws or body.

The easiest way to clip your Bichon Frise is to do a puppy cut. This is the same length all over.

For the show-ring, the Bichon Frise can be clipped like a poodle or with a long puffy coat; feet and muzzle clipped. As you can see by the picture, it makes for a great look.

Your pet is known for its merry and jolly nature. This shows up in the jaunty plumed tail carried over the back and the dark bright eyes.

Your dog is probably 9 ½ and 11 ½ inches tall. But don't worry if he or she is a little over or under that. Compact and proportionately made, the Bichon Frise will stand proud and happy at your side, in your arms and your lap, wherever you go.

A healthy Bichon Frise has an expression of soft, dark-eyed, inquisitiveness. He is always alert! The black or very dark brown skin that surrounds the eyes – known as halos – accentuates the eye and enhances the expression. The eye rims are black. The nose is always black. The lips are also black and fine.

Your Bichon Frise carries his head proudly on a long, arched neck that smoothly blends into the shoulders.

Coat texture is an extremely important factor. The undercoat should be soft and dense, the outer coat coarse and curly. This combination results in a coat that is soft and substantial, similar to plush or velvet which, when patted, will spring back. When bathed and brushed, the hair stands off the body, creating an overall powder-puff look.

Remember to trim your little friend to reveal the body's natural outline. It's never cut so short as to be overly trimmed or squared off, but should be rounded off from any direction. Fringes about the head, beard, moustache, ears and tail are left longer. Longer head hair is trimmed so as to create an overall rounded impression. The topline should appear level. Overall, the coat should be long enough to maintain that powder-puff look that is the breed's signature characteristic.

When your Bichon Frise moves at a trot, it should be free, precise and effortless. The forelegs and hind legs should extend equally with an easy reach and drive that maintain a steady topline when viewed in profile. The head and neck stay somewhat erect and as speed increases there will be a very slight convergence of the legs toward the center line. Moving away from the viewer, the hindquarters travel with a moderate width between them and footpads can be seen. Whether coming or going, the movement should be precise and true. A true beauty, your dog can maintain this in the show ring, but whether jumping into your lap or bouncing across the room, he's a real beauty.

History

The Bichon Frise descends in ancestry from the Barbet or Water Spaniel. Thus came the name "Barbichon," which was later shortened to "Bichon." The Bichons were then divided into four categories: Bichon Maltais, Bichon Bolognais, Bichon Havanais and Bichon Teneriffe – all originating in the Mediterranean area.

With their merry disposition, they travelled much and were used as barter by sailors from continent to continent. They found early success in Spain where it is generally believed Spanish seamen introduced them to the Canary Island of Teneriffe. In the 1300's, Italian sailors rediscovered the little dogs and returned them to the Continent, where they soon became great favorites of the Italian nobility. As was common in those days, court dogs were trimmed "lion style" leaving a huge mane about the head, a shortly cropped body, and a ball of tuff at the end of the tail.

The "Teneriffe" or "Bichon" became popular in France during the Renaissance under Francis (1515-1547) and skyrocketed into even more popularity in Henry III's court (1574-89). The breed continued successfully in Spain as a favorite of the Infantas. Spanish painters often included them in their works. The famous artist, Goya, for example, included a Bichon in several of his paintings.

Though already popular in France, the interest grew further during the reign of Napoleon III, then waned until the late 1800's when it became the "common dog," running the streets, accompanying organ grinders of Barbary, leading the blind and performing in circuses and fairs.

March 5, 1933 – the Societe Centrale Canine of France adopted the official breed standard. Since the breed was known by two names, "Teneriffe" and "Bichon," the President of the International Canine Federation proposed a name based on the dog's characteristics – the Bichon Frise ("Frise" refers to the dog's soft curly hair). The French Kennel Club admitted the Bichon Frise to the stud book on October 18, 1934.

The U.S. recorded its first Bichon litter when it was whelped in 1956. Two other breeders in different parts of the U.S. acquired Bichons in 1959 and 1960. Thus began the origins for the breed's development in this country.

It wasn't until September 1, 1971 that the Bichon Frise became eligible to enter the Miscellaneous Class. Shortly after, in October, 1972, the breed was admitted for registration in the American Kennel Club Stud Book. The breed then became eligible to show in the Non-Sporting Group at AKC dog shows on April 4, 1973.

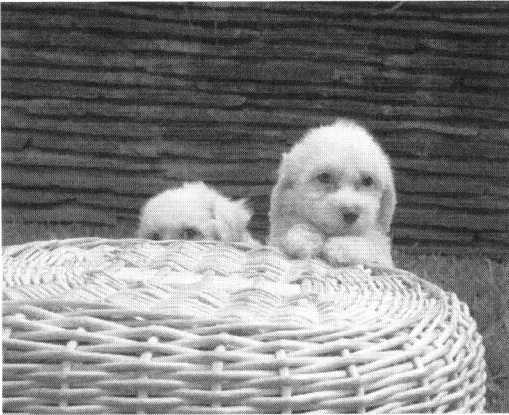

Temperament of the dog

The Bichon Frise is referred to as "merry" and "cheerful" by The American Kennel Club (AKC). The standard requires a dog be "gentle mannered, sensitive, playful and affectionate". The fluffy, little white dog has an independent spirit, is intelligent, bold and lively. He's not a yapper and has an even happy temperament that's easy to live with. The Bichon Frise loves human company and will demand much attention. They are sociable and thrive with a family that takes them everywhere. Because they are so playful and have lots of energy, they do well with children. Bred as companion dogs, the Bichon Frise gets along with children and other animals. In other words, he's the best all-around pet for your needs He can fit easily into most any family situation, and will give you hours of love and affection.

They are bright little dogs, easy to train, and love everyone. They need people to be happy. Used as watchdogs and to perform tricks, the Bichon Frise is competitive and obedient. Like a lot of smaller breeds, the Bichon may be hard to housebreak. He needs rules to follow and limits to what he's allowed or not allowed to do. They also need a daily walk. Whatever you do, don't let this little dog develop what is called "Small Dog Syndrome" – a human induced behavior that sets him up as pack leader to humans. This can cause a wide variety of behavioral problems included, but not limited to, obsessive barking, guarding, and separation anxiety, snapping and even biting. These aren't Bichon traits, but rather behaviors brought on by the treatment of the dog. If you start out as your dog's pack leader and stay consistently self-assured, calm and assertive, providing daily walks and so on, the Bichon will be a stable-minded and trustworthy dog. I'm sure you'll want to give your dog the best of his needs for you as his pack leader as this will make you both happiest together.

Potential ailments as a puppy and health issues as it matures.

Have to discuss the serious stuff here if you're taking on a puppy. Some Bichons are prone to watery eyes, cataracts, skin and ear ailments, epilepsy and dislocated kneecaps. They can be sensitive to flea bites.

Bichon Frise in (combined) UK and USA/Canada surveys have an average life span of about 12–13 years, with Bichon Frises in the UK tending to live longer than Bichon Frises in the US/Canada. This breed's longevity is similar to other breeds of its size, and somewhat longer than purebred dogs in general. The longest lived of 34 deceased Bichons in a 2004 UK survey died at 16.5 years.

The oldest Bichon Frises for which there are reliable records in various US/Canada surveys have died at 19 years. We want you to have the best of your years together with your Bichon Frise and for those years to be the best for him. We know you're looking forward to it, too.

Be on the lookout for symptoms that indicate your Bichon might have liver shunts. These are common in some small breeds. These often go undetected until later in life, leading to complications that can't be fixed and therefore liver failure. Bichons who are underweight, runts of the litter, or have negative reactions to food high in protein are likely to be suffering from a shunt. When detected early, shunts can often be corrected through surgery. However, the later in life the shunt is detected, the lower the likelihood of surgery being a success. Shunts can be kept under control through special diets of low protein and through medications to support liver function, help flush toxins that build up in the kidneys and liver, and control seizures that often occur as a symptom of the shunt. Without surgery, Bichons with shunts live to be 4–6 years old. Owners of a smaller-than-average-size Bichon must consult a vet. Other symptoms include dark urine, lethargy, loss of appetite, an increase in drinking. Seizures come in all forms; episodes of seizures can begin early on but go undetected. Early seizures can appear to put the Bichon in a hypnotic state (staring at something not there), or to be experiencing an episode of vertigo, or being drunk. Shunts are a serious condition of smaller breeds, and often not associated with Bichons.

Bichon Frise dogs are generally quite healthy. It is important to go through a reputable breeder and to consult your veterinarian about health information. Puppy mills and many backyard breeders will produce and sell puppies that have numerous health problems. Well-bred dogs of this breed, fortunately, have few health concerns.

The most common health problems affecting Bichons are not usually life-threatening. The most common problem encountered in this breed, as in other white dogs, is allergic reactions. These issues usually manifest themselves in dogs as skin problems, such as itching. Most of the time, a veterinarian can help to instruct you to keep these problems under control with shampoos and topical creams. More severe cases sometimes require steroid medications. Not much different from certain people who get skin rashes or who are allergic to certain plants and insects.

Bichons can also suffer from a problem that commonly affects small dogs - tooth decay. This can start as a minor problem, but if let go, can be very harmful to the health of your dog. Regular care, such as brushing of teeth, with periodic dental cleanings, can prevent this issue and is an important part of owning a Bichon.

Bichons, like other dogs with floppy ears, are also prone to yeast in the ears. You will find this condition prevalent during the Spring. The yeast looks dark like grease mixed with dirt. A visit to the vet for a prescription can solve this issue. There is a similar problem and that is the stained hair from runny eyes. Do not be alarmed. Your dog's tears contain chemicals that react with sunlight. This is usually a cosmetic problem and can be minimized by clipping the hair close to the face or cleaning the area with a diluted solution of Hydrogen Peroxide (Caution: do not get the solution in your dog's eye).

Other problems occasionally seen in the breed are an autoimmune disorder affecting the lungs, and cancer in older dogs. However, you could say that cancer in old dogs is common to all breeds. Patellar luxation (slippage of the kneecaps in the hind legs) also sometimes affects this breed. A healthy Bichon can live 14-16 years. Some dogs have lived as many as 18 years.

What a new owner can expect

You have to realize that deciding to own and raise a pedigreed dog is not a "paint by numbers" job. Each breed will have its unique nature, quirks, and characteristics.

You may not know exactly what to expect with your new Bichon Frise addition, but by researching, you can have a general idea of what to do in the days, weeks, and months following your pup's arrival. Just remember, although the following lists out the specifics of your dog's care, what he needs most from you that will include everything else, is lots of love and affection, well-mixed with the right kind of discipline that helps him be the best he can be for you and for himself! Have fun!

F.Y.B.F.I. (For Your Bichon Frise Information)—

Yes, your Bichon Frise is completely unique and has a personality all his or her own. Even so, just as there are general guidelines for taking care of a baby, here are a few basic similarities in the breed that most, if not all Bichons will exhibit:

- They do not like to be left alone for long periods. A Bichon left alone for more than a few hours on a regular basis can develop separation anxiety, which could mean chewed shoes.

- Bichons can be hard to housebreak. Be sure to stock up on puppy pads, Bounty, and patience. A kennel can help, too.

- They love attention. Expect to see those two sparkling eyes and nose up-close often. It's a good thing Bichon Frise dogs do not shed, or you would be covered in white hair.

- They are watchdogs, and will be kind enough to alert you to any guests, mailmen, paperboys, visiting squirrels, and unique cloud formations.

- There is a lot of home grooming needed so your Bichon Frise looks, and feels velvety soft. If you are not able to brush his or her coat out once a day, it should be done at least twice a week. Otherwise, the coat will become matted and tangled.

- Professional grooming visits are highly suggested every four or five weeks. Consider it a spa day for your pup.

- Bichons can be stubborn, but they are known to respond very well to training; especially when treats are involved. Of course, that could also describe a lot of humans.

- Your Bichon Frise is a lively entertainer. They love to learn new tricks and show them off. Don't forget those treats!

A lot of how your puppy responds to you depends on how they've been treated before they arrive in your home. No animals acts out without reason and Bichons are no different. If they are withdrawn and/or edgy there is most certainly a reason why. Be well researched and picky about which Bichon Frise breeders you purchase from. There are tips and information you should know before even making a phone call.

Puppy Proofing Your Home and Yard

It's very important for your new puppy's safety and well-being that you prepare for his homecoming by "puppy proofing" your house. Get down on your puppy's level – on your hands and knees. Crawl and look around each room to see what your puppy could get into. Look for things like electrical cords, poisonous plants; anything that your puppy could chew or swallow, and anything else that could cause your puppy harm. If you have valuable furniture or special items in your home you don't want damaged, move the item out of reach or put it away until your puppy is older. Examples of favorite things to chew on are throw rugs, toys and newspapers (or the mail)! If you can't afford to have it destroyed, get it out of pup's way. And remember - anything swallowed that can't pass through the pup's system will require surgery to remove. By the way, holiday time is the worst time to bring a puppy home for this and other reasons!

It's best to buy child safety gates to secure your pup in a room that is a safe environment. Select a room where you can watch him all the time. If you aren't watching your puppy, put him into his kennel or exercise pen. (Exercise pens can be purchased from venders of pet products.) Follow this procedure until your puppy has finished his teething stage and is 100% housetrained for at least 2 weeks or more. Yes, that means several months. Remember, patience – like silence – can be golden.

If there are items that you do NOT want to move and your puppy just can't resist chewing them, you can use a chew repellant spray. You can get these at most any pet store, from a catalog, or even online. Some are better than others, so you may have to try a few before finding that 'right' one that works. Adding a firm "No" (not harsh) is a great way to start obedience training. You'll be surprised how fast he learns! Cause he truly wants to please!

Some of the things you may miss while puppy proofing are garbage and trash cans in the kitchen, bedrooms and baths. Baby locks are great to prevent access to under counter cabinets. Open trash cans should be placed high in rooms, out of pup's reach. If you forget that, you'll only do it once, I assure you. It's amazing how much damage that cute powder-puff can do! Just as children need boundaries (well, we all do actually), so does your Bichon Frise. He'll behave much better for it. And you'll have more peace of mind.

Some of the greatest hazards to a pup are home exits! Bichons are very fast and often mischievous, so doors should be carefully closed and children *must* be taught not to hold a door open, or the pup will escape. A fenced yard is imperatively important before some breeders will even consider placing a pup. Be sure to add the words "Sit" and "Stay" to your repertoire of early training, and require the pup to be in position before opening the door once he's learned these commands.

Walk the entire fence line – more than once. Look for loose or broken boards that might provide an easy escape route for your puppy. Make sure there are no gaps under the fence that a dog can slip through. Even a space as small as 2-5 inches can allow a young dog to get free. And remember, dogs dig! Check the gate latches each and every time someone enters or leaves the yard to be certain they're always secured. Make sure everyone, from children to gardeners and even family visitors know to close and latch each gate every time they enter or leave the property. This is extremely important to the safety and protection of your new puppy! If you're unsure at all about your fence and gates being able to confine your puppy, then NEVER let him out in your backyard without being on a leash or being supervised. You can even set up a large safe play area by putting two exercise pens together and putting them either on your patio, lawn or a combination of both. Even then, supervision is important because some Bichons are great climbers.

Take extra care if you have a swimming pool that the puppy might fall into. Swimming pools are natural temptations to a curious pup. Even if the same pup hates having a bath! He may not realize he can't walk on water, or he may accidentally fall in while playing. It's always a good idea to teach your puppy how to get out of a pool in case he does fall in – so he won't drown. Not all dogs are natural swimmers. When it's time to give your puppy a bath, go with him for a swim first. Pool chemicals are harmful to his coat and need to be shampooed out anyway. Show him how to get out of the pool safely. This goes for large ponds or any body of water nearby. Afterwards, give him a complete bath to get rid of all the chemicals. It's a good idea to repeat the swimming pool lesson at least annually so your Bichon remembers how to get out of a pool if he falls in.

Some plants can be poisonous to dogs. If you're not certain if the plant your puppy just shredded is poisonous, you can look up a listing of poisonous plants that are poisonous to dogs on the internet. Remember, every minute counts if your puppy's been poisoned! Contact your vet immediately!

Get rid of any and all fleas and ticks you may have in your home or on your property before you bring a puppy home. It's always easier to maintain a flea-free puppy if the puppy doesn't have fleas in the first place. A few weeks before you're scheduled to pick up the little darling, have your home and yard sprayed for fleas and ticks. If you already have pets, make sure all of them are flea-free, too. Outside cats are terrific flea attractants. If necessary, have your other pets dipped. Do NOT bring your new puppy into a flea-ridden environment since some Bichons are extremely allergic to fleabites.

Ok, here's a little unpleasant topic and we might as well get out of the way, since it's as much a hazard to your mental well-being as to the puppy's health. Dogs (young and old) are sometimes "poop eaters." Some Bichons are guilty of this nasty habit. Sure, there are products you can get from vets to discourage it, but they rarely work. The only sure way to prevent it is to follow up behind your dog and pick up what's been deposited. Needless to say, that should be done anyway for sanitation's sake. Nobody knows why this happens and it doesn't seem to harm the dog, but don't be surprised if your sweet cutesy little Bichon has a little "dessert" now and then.

Another real hazard is the danger of a fire while you're away from home. Most fire companies – and other sources – have stickers (called "pet locators") that can be attached to a window or door where a pet can be found while you're away. Inside, in his crate or kennel and taking a nap is where he can be safe, content and easily found should the unexpected happen.

Above all else, enjoy your puppy in the warm, safe home you've made for him. If you feel your home and yard are "child proof," it's a good bet your puppy is safe there, too. Remember to keep a close eye on your puppy when you first bring him home just in case you missed something dangerous to his safety.

And one final word of warning (I know, I'm beginning to sound like your Dad or Mom, right?), NEVER leave your puppy in the backyard when you're not at home to supervise him. You could come home to find him missing or badly injured. Take care to ensure his safety whether you're at home or away. Here in Texas, we have Coyotes, Owls and other natural predators in our area that would treat your dog as prey. Please be mindful of the natural predators in your area that would be a threat to your dog when they're outside.

Care and maintenance of the Bison Frise

You'll want to groom this breed a lot and bathe him every month. Professional grooming should happen every four weeks. The hair around the eyes and ears can be trimmed with a blunt pair of scissors. Clean the eyes to prevent staining. Trim a show dog with scissors. You can use electric clippers on the body of pet dogs, but scissors for the rest. The Bichon sheds little to no hair and is good for allergy sufferers.

A daily walk is a necessity for these active little dogs. Play takes care of a lot of their exercise needs, but will not fulfill their need to walk. Behavioral problems can crop up when a dog doesn't get a daily walk. They also love a good romp in a safe, open area off-leash, like a large fenced-in yard.

Because of their need for lots of grooming, a Bichon Frise is known as a high maintenance dog. Most pet owners depend on a professional groomer to do the major bath and haircut that is needed once a month. It takes time and practice to master those grooming techniques. There are many tasks to be done at home between those monthly visits. We will discuss all those and how they should be done plus list the tools needed for keeping his coat, teeth, toenails and pads in good shape. BFCA also provides a booklet, *Your Bichon Frise,* which you can order for complete information on home grooming.

Tools Needed:
- A coarse-medium greyhound-type comb
- Pin brush
- Slicker brush
- Scissors (specifically for dog grooming)
- Blunt tip tweezers
- Toenail clippers
- Styptic for treating bleeding toenails.
- Toothbrush, paste and scalers (see article on Dental Care)

Note: You'll also need a hair dryer if you bathe the dog at home.

Buy quality tools as cheap ones will destroy the coat.

Daily:
Two of the most important daily tasks are brushing and combing through the coat to prevent matting and daily care of the teeth. You can read more about dental care in the article mentioned above.

An adult Bichon's coat is a double coat. That means there are both soft hairs and a coarser type of hair, called guard hairs. Guard hairs are not present at birth. They start to show up along the lower back just before the dog's first birthday. A young pup doesn't mat, but you'll want to start him on a daily combing to train him to accept this attention and establish this daily habit early in his life. Begin by brushing through his coat with the pin brush. This will remove the small knots of beginning mats. Then you can comb through his hair for the final touch-up. You can find brushing instructions below. While brushing, be on the lookout for fleas, sores, lumps or any other changes that might need veterinary care.

Just before his adult coat comes in, his hair will begin to mat very easily. Though the Bichon doesn't shed, he (like his human owner) has a lot of dead hair that must be removed to prevent matting. In fact, it's because he doesn't shed the dead hair that it has to be combed and brushed out. The closer he gets to his double coat, the worse this will become to the point he may need combing out twice a day! Dead hair will form mats that, if neglected, become like felt. To remove them will require one of two drastic measures. He'll either have to be shaved to the skin or the mats broken up and removed, one by one. That is a very painful process. Groomers charge more for a matted dog, since there is more work involved, so it's in your best interest to avoid that happening, as well as the dog's.

Weekly:
Check the teeth for tartar and remove as needed.
See *The Importance of Good Dental Care in a Bichon* for instructions.

Check his pads and toenails. Hair around the toe pads should be trimmed away with scissors. This is where the blunt-nosed scissors come in handy. Don't forget to remove any hair from between the pads, too. This hair can collect debris that will form rock-like knots if not removed regularly. Plus keeping the pads free of hair helps the dog maintain traction and prevents sore feet.

Clip toenails at least every other week. Check for the pink vein that runs the length of the toenail and cut just below the vein. If bleeding occurs, even from your best efforts, use a styptic to stop it. You can have your groomer or vet show you how to properly clip them.

Monthly:
As I mentioned before, the dog should be bathed and trimmed at least once a month. It's ok to bathe him more often and many owners schedule this for every two weeks. Emergency baths can be given (at home or by the groomer). Just be sure to first brush out any knots or mats. Wetting those mats just makes the knots tighter. If you bathe him at home, use a shampoo for white dogs and rinse thoroughly. Human shampoos have the wrong pH for a dog and leaving soap in the coat can be harmful to the coat and may affect the skin.

Brushing the dog:
Train your dog to lie on his side in order to get a proper brushing of his coat. The basic idea is to brush the hair up from the skin, not down or flat against the skin. Brush the hair on his head toward the face, taking care

not to stick the dog's eye with the brush. Brush the dog's sides upward toward the spine while he's lying on his side. Carefully work out any mats or knots, using the end tooth of the comb. The best way to do this is to work the knot from the tip furthest from the skin, gently pulling and working the knot loose from outward in. To say the least, the sooner you discover a knot and work it loose, the easier it will be to remove it. Large mats take infinite patience and lots of time to break up.

The ears, tail and legs comes next. Mats are most likely to form on the legs, especially on a dog that tends to chew or lick himself. Like the body, brush the leg hair up and out from the skin. When brushing the ears, start with the underside first, then work on the outer side. Since the ears and tail have longer hair, work on the ends first and get them tangle-free. Slowly move the brush up an inch or so nearer the body until there are no more tangles and you can freely pull the brush the length of the hair from the skin outward. There are spray products available to help untangle hair. Spray the area; work the spray into the coat, then brush.

Take care when using the end tooth of the comb while working out the knots. You don't want to injury the skin, especially on older dogs. Avoid getting sprays or shampoo in the eyes, and be careful not to poke them with the comb or brush. While bathing your dog, keep water out of the ear canal by putting a bit of cotton in the ear during the bath.

The same technique you use for brushing your dog before a bath applies to brushing out his wet coat after a bath. Towel him as dry as you possibly can, then brush him free of any mats you might have missed prior to bathing. The final touch comes with drying off with a hair dryer, while at the same time brushing and straightening out the curl to get that powder-puff look of the Bichon. Hot air can burn your dog's skin, so use a cooler setting! This is when you'll use the slicker brush. So, it goes like this:

1. Use the pin brush and comb on dry coat or immediately after the bath to work out knots.
2. Use the slicker brush as a finishing brush to finish removing the curl.

The slicker brush is NOT for removing tangles because it will pull too much undercoat out and leave the beautiful plush coat thin and sparse. For more detail on bathing, drying and trimming procedures, see *Your Bichon Frise* or another booklet or video on grooming.

Many pet owners don't understand how the Bichon trim should look. There are drawings and explanations in the booklet that will help you. Even if you're having your Bichon professionally groomed, you may want to refer to our BFCA Photo Gallery. There you'll see pictures of adults and puppies. While a puppy or adult can have shorter haircuts, the general outline and appearance of the newly groomed Bichon should look much the same as these photos. The tail remains long and flowing; ears, beard and moustache kept short, but not shaved or overly trimmed. The Bichon Frise is a unique breed unto itself and your pet shouldn't be trimmed to look like any other breed. This isn't a poodle mix or a kind of terrier but a "white powder-puff of a dog." Proper grooming will make him look exactly as he should, whether he's in full show coat or a shorter pet trim.

Feeding

If you bought your Bichon from a responsible breeder, you were given written instructions on the care and feeding of the puppy. This section doesn't intend to override those instructions. However, many pups are sent home with minimal instructions. This information is provided to assist you in getting your pup off to a good start and to guide you in providing healthy food.

What to feed the Bichon Frise:
Always provide premium dog food and avoid generic brands. Premium pet foods haven't always been available at grocery stores, but that's changed in recent years. Some brands are better for your pet than others. We don't offer specific brand names, but you can go by price. Generally, the cheaper food indicates a poorer quality of ingredients. Ask your local pet supply store for a list of premium foods and choose from among them. Until your dog is a year old, this means a Puppy formula.

The premium foods are based on serious research that says that a dry (kibble) diet is better for a dog's health. Dry food is better for dental health (see *The Importance of Good Dental Care in a Bichon*), and the kibble diet is balanced with vitamins, minerals and ratio of fat to protein to carbohydrates. As such, there's never a reason to add other foods, including canned dog food. In fact, adding other foods can upset the important balance of minerals and vitamins and can lead to obesity over time. An occasional treat will be discussed later.

The food you feed your puppy affects his future health:
What a dog eats can affect their future health in relation to allergies, weight and general overall health. Starting him out with quality foods can have a life-long effect. Some of the ingredients you'll want to see in his dog food are meat – not meat byproducts, cereals such as barley, brown rice and oatmeal, natural additives and vitamins, probiotics/lactobacillus, vegetables (not just corn and beets), and natural preservatives instead of chemicals. The dietary ingredients will sound a lot like a human diet and will be balanced. If you buy from a pet food supplier, you'll be able to talk to an employee knowledgeable about quality dog foods. A grocery clerk won't have that kind of knowledge and most grocers don't carry premium foods. Premium foods cost more, but the extra cost is well-balanced against the veterinary costs that will be encountered later in life from feeding low-quality brands of food.

When to give treats:
Treats are used in training your puppy. You can find a lot of information to instruct you about using treats for training. If you feel you must use treats to say "I love you", use a piece of the daily allotted amount of kibble or rarely offer a tiny bit of lean chicken. In fact, his kibble is the best treat for training, as well. Deduct the treats from the total amount fed daily. Remember that what you feed today may affect your puppy later in life! This includes over-feeding. Obesity adds stress to hips and knees and may set the dog up for pancreatitis, diabetes and other metabolic problems.

When and how much to feed:
Hopefully you haven't purchased a puppy as young as 6 weeks old. He's just being weaned and is nowhere near ready to leave the litter. A responsible breeder won't place pups younger than 10-13 weeks of age. However we know that pups are shipped from mass breeding kennels as early as 8 weeks and we take that into consideration in providing this schedule. Remember that the total amount of food in a 24 hour period for a normal sized Bichon is about 1 cup of dry kibble. The following schedule is based on that total amount. Be sure to remove any uneaten food after 10 minutes.

A schedule for feeding:
Pups just weaned must eat four meals a day.   These meals should be about 4-5 hours apart. Divide the cup of food into four portions and give him the first ¼ cup when he wakes up in the morning - after he has been

walked. The next ¼ cup will be about midday, followed by a third ¼ cup in the late afternoon, say between 5-6 PM. A final feeding will be given in the evening. Read *Crate Training Your Puppy* to understand how this works into the house training schedule.

Starting at 10 weeks of age, watch the puppy for signs that he may be ready to cut the number of meals to 3 times a day. When he starts to leave some of his food at the second meal, try him at 3 meals a day. Adjust the following schedule to your schedule:

6-8 AM Feed 1/3 cup of dry kibble; midday feed 1/3 cup of dry kibble and about 6 PM feed 1/3 cup of dry kibble. You may want to set aside just a few pieces of kibble for bedtime but a full meal at bedtime will probably cause him to need to go outside during the night. Review *Crate Training Your Puppy* for more information on training him to be clean in the house.

If he won't eat the dry food:
Moisten the food for a few days until you are sure he is eating well and then gradually reduce the amount of water added until he is eating dry kibble. Try giving him dry food at first and only add water if he won't eat it dry. Don't add any other food to the dry kibble. It may take a couple of days to adapt to his new food. You can always alternate between wet and dry for a short time but it is to his and your advantage for him to eat it dry.

When to switch to one or two meals a day:
At some point, around six months of age, he won't want all his food at midday. At this time, change the amount given to 1/2 cup of dry kibble and feed him twice a day. Suggested meal times would be 7-8 AM and 6-8 PM. Most Bichons do well on two meals a day for the rest of their lives. Switch to adult formula at about one year of age. Change to a Senior formula after age seven or so.

Feeding in his kennel is a good thing. Puppies fed in their kennels will more readily accept being in the kennel. This also assures that each pet, in multi-pet households, eats only his own food. This is very important in controlling weight gain. When introducing a pet the first time to a kennel, throw a piece of kibble into the crate as a treat.

Talking about meat and vegetables:
A balanced premium dry food provides your Bichon with all the nutrients he needs for a healthy life. If you do decide to occasionally give him a tidbit of lean meat, cooked egg, yogurt or a treat of raw apple or carrot, it won't upset his nutritional balance. The treats should be given in relation to his size. A 12-14 pound dog doesn't need a Great Dane sized portion so we're talking about a teaspoon or less of supplemental food. There's another issue: dogs with calcium bladder stones or with metabolic or other diseases can be harmed when you add the wrong food to his diet. Just be sure you don't get carried away with extras. We want to remind you that obesity in dogs is a huge problem these days. This can increase his chances of patellar luxation, diabetes, pancreatitis and other conditions.

So instead of extra meat, should I give him vitamins?
The answer to that question is NO!
Remember, you want a balanced diet from his premium dog food. If you add vitamins and minerals to that diet, you'd be throwing off the research proven balance for a growing puppy (or for a healthy adult). A sick dog may need some sort of prescribed supplement, but a healthy dog does not. Your veterinarian will tell you if he needs something special added to his daily diet. We hope he stays healthy and does not ever have to have prescribed medications or vitamin supplements.

Suppose I did not feed my Bichon this way from the start and now he wants his food mixed with meat. What do you suggest?
Finicky eaters are created and, with patience, they can be trained out of their bad habits. Gradually cut down the amount of meat you add to his dry food until there is none added. If he won't eat the food after 10 or 15 minutes, pick it up and offer no more food until the next scheduled feeding time. Do this at each meal for a few days and he will eat – so long as you do not give him treats in between. Of course he will need water and his water bowl should be available all the time.

The breeder of my puppy gave me instructions for a diet based on raw foods. Is this a good diet?
There are diets available that include raw foods and some dedicated pet owners follow those diets. There is absolutely nothing wrong with these diets, but they take a lot of time to prepare. For the person who devotes the necessary time, who has access to the raw products and who is

consistent in following this diet plan, these diets are very healthy for the dog. However, this is not a dietary plan that works conveniently for humans. It takes dedication, research, study, shopping for quality ingredients, and a home freezer for storage – and so on. If you work full time, have a family who needs your time and attention, tend to be a bit disorganized; we can't, in all honesty, recommend that you start this kind of diet plan. For that reason, we suggest PREMIUM prepared dog foods as the answer to feeding your Bichon.

However, if your dog is your family and you want to provide quality human grade food, this is the route to take. Be certain to do justice in consistently providing quality ingredients. Study the diets and follow them accurately. There are a number of publications available to help you.

Always provide fresh water that is readily available to the puppy or adult. Fresh available water is essential to good health

FOODS YOU SHOULD NEVER FEED YOUR DOG
- Alcohol
- Apple cores (seeds are poisonous)
- Cooked bones (they splinter)
- Caffeine
- Chocolate
- Raw dough
- Garlic
- Grapes
- Moldy foods, including aged cheeses
- Mushrooms
- Onions
- Raisins

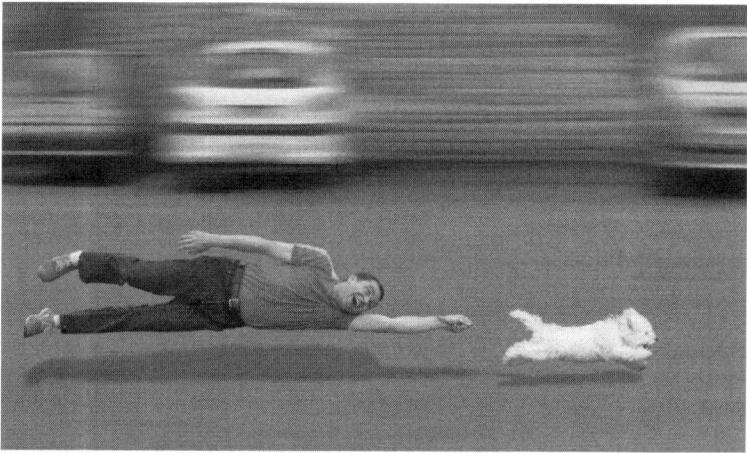

Training i.e. house, obedience, barking etc.

The intelligent, friendly, and attention-loving Bichon is a relatively easy dog to train. They are eager and willing. They are also sensitive, so harsh corrective training methods are not suited to this breed. They respond extremely well to positive, rewards-based methods, and will quickly pick up tricks and basic commands. I suggest using the clicker training techniques when training your Bichon. A clicker is very effective.

One behavior that shouldn't be encouraged is called "Small Dog Syndrome". This happens when owners treat their cute little pets more like dolls or babies than like dogs. Constant cuddling and carrying the dog around creates a nervous, anxious, snappish animal that constantly challenges people. The Bichon is an adorable little dog. Just be aware not to treat it as a fragile toy.

As with most small dogs, housetraining can take a bit more effort. Be prepared with a consistent routine of frequent potty breaks, and always use positive reinforcement for your puppy. It isn't true that small dogs can't be housebroken. It takes awareness that their tiny bladders need frequent relief. The younger the dog, the more attention they will need in this area.

There are a few methods that are very helpful in training. As with any dog, basic commands like "sit," "down," "recall" (come) and "leave-it" will give you and your pet a good foundation for nice behavior and safety. It's important to teach the Bichon to walk on a loose leash, and to use a harness. Their tiny neck and throat can be harmed by straining and pulling.

The cheerful and friendly Bichon Frise is a joy to train and have as a member of the household. They are beautiful little dogs.

How to Housebreak a Bichon Frise:
The Bichon Frise is on a Top 10 List of "Hard to Housebreak." Consistent kennel training is mandatory. Sometimes a doggy door is necessary, and it should lead out to a COVERED potty yard, as Bichons often won't go out in the rain. Housebreaking issues are a major reason why Bichons are turned over to rescue organizations.

1 – Wake up early to start training your Bichon Frise. These high-energy pups will grasp the concept of housebreaking more easily if you can catch them before their first indoor accident. Rise around 6:00 am (or whatever time your puppy gets going) and begin the training outdoors.

2 – Use one-word commands whenever possible. The housebreaking command can be anything you want, but "outside" is recommended. The one-word command keeps the dog's attention. This is especially important since this breed is easily distracted. Repeat your one-word command in a kind, encouraging tone until your Bichon Frise relieves itself outdoors.

3 – Praise your puppy when it finishes its "business." Bichons can read the tone of your voice. In turn, hearing a stern, sharp tone when it has an accident will let it know it has disappointed you.

4 – Repeat the process within the hour, after feeding times and when you see your puppy drink a significant amount of water. Remember, this breed is overloaded with energy, so it may take a while to get your point across and meet success with some regularity. Be patient.

5 – Continue to praise and reward the Bichon Frise every time it relieves itself in an appropriate location. Be consistent in praise and punishment until it is fully housebroken.

Tips & Warnings

Housebreaking a Bichon is difficult, but worth it. They are loveable, fun dogs and terrific companions.

Expect mistakes. Even if your Bichon has been a straight-A housebreaking student, don't be surprised if he makes a mistake, or even regresses for a short while. Continue with consistency and praise.

Successfully housebreaking your Bichon takes a lot of time and patience. If you are unable to invest this kind of time, then this isn't the right breed for you.

KEY WORD: Consistency!
Some people have said Bichons, Shih-Tzu and other small dogs are impossible to housebreak. We disagree! If you can train an owner, you can train any dog at any age. Here is the best method:

Don't free-feed a dog that is not housebroken. Put your dog on a feeding schedule: Breakfast and dinner. Mix about 1 TBS add in (canned food, yogurt, cottage cheese, canned pumpkin, hamburger & rice) with dry food. **NOTE*** quality dog food is essential in housebreaking. Poor quality dog food can cause digestive problems and make housebreaking a nightmare! NutriSource products are excellent choices (www.NutriSourceDogFood.com). By adding add-ins to the dry, you will help your dog process his meal faster and he will void regularly. A dog that is a "nibbler" from free-feeding is much harder to housebreak. Do not feed or water after dinner time. Your dog will go to bed with a mostly empty bladder and bowel and should sleep through the night without an accident.

Take your dog out about 45 minutes after he eats to void out his meal. Use your usual command each time you take him out so he knows the purpose of his visit to the outdoors. If he does not void right away, get him moving around by playing with him as this will help get those bowels moving. If he still doesn't void, take him inside and put him in his kennel. Allow another 10-15 minutes and try again. DO NOT LET YOUR DOG LOOSE IF HE HAS NOT GONE POTTY! He will void on your floor.

Take your dog out every 2 hours to pee. Use the same encouragement and command. When your dog wakes up from a nap and first thing in the morning, he will have to go. Quickly take him out to do so.

When you take your dog out to void, go with him. He wants to be with you, and if you just put him out and leave him, he will stand at the door waiting for you. He will then void the minute you let him in. You need to go with him. Every time your dog voids as he should, give him lots of praise and a treat. This will reinforce that he's doing something good.

Keep a diary the first couple weeks to note when your dog voids. This will help you know his schedule. He will be very consistent and that will help with the training!

Use your kennel wisely! It is the best training tool you will own. When you leave for a couple hours put your dog in its kennel. Always use it for bedtime. Make sure you do not feed him at bedtime though, or you are asking for an accident! If you're going to be gone for over 4 hours (2 hours with a young puppy), do not use your kennel. It's physically impossible for him to hold it that long, and to ask him to do so could cause future health issues. In the case where you're gone for extended periods of time, and for those who work during the day, gate off a laundry or kitchen area where he can have his kennel or a soft bed to sleep in, and a place to void. Use pee pads or a litter box for this extended absence need.

Don't leave an un-housebroken dog free in the house. It's not fair to him or yourself as he's certain to have accidents.

It's important for you to encourage him with positive praise when he voids correctly and keep a consistent schedule until he is housebroken. If you're not consistent, your dog won't know what to do, and you'll find training next to impossible. If necessary, use a timer to remind yourself that it's potty time. If you have children, make sure everyone is in on the schedule and everyone is doing the same thing. DO NOT use multiple ways to train – i.e. litter box and outside. This will only confuse your dog. Bichon Frise dogs are very smart. They will learn quickly and easily with praise, treats and a structured schedule.

If an adult dog (male or female) is a "marker" - peeing on things like furniture, grocery bags, purses on floors, etc. use a doggie diaper for the dog while in the house until housebroken. This won't help housebreak your dog, but it will protect your carpet and furniture from pee stains while training. In some cases, dog diapers can help housebreak as the dog may not like the moisture on his own body when he potties. Also, with a "marker," a spray bottle (or put pennies in a can and shake) will be your best friend while training. When your dog goes to "mark" something, that is his/her way of saying "This is Mine!" You have to teach him that it is NOT his. You do this by taking the spray bottle (or put pennies in a can and shake) and spray the dog while saying "NO! BAD DOG!" Put your dog in time-out in his kennel for a few minutes. Afterwards, take him outside and tell him to go potty using the same command you have already been using. Dogs will normally "mark territory" when they feel insecure about their life – i.e. a rescue who hasn't had a home of his own, or an existing pet in the course of a move, divorce, or other family upset. Marking is a bad habit, and bad habits can be broken. The spray bottle, (pennies in the can) and stern command will turn this around.

What about paper training? This is a decision you must make early on. If it is a male, he probably should never be paper trained. Females can learn to go outside as well as on papers and this can be useful in parts of the country with bad winters. The papers must - from the start - only be placed in an area where they will continue to be permissible, usually a laundry room.

Occasionally there will be a male that is exceptionally hard to housetrain. Neutering him will help. The earlier a male is neutered, the less likely he is to lift his leg so do this around 6 months of age. When he is out of his kennel, you can "diaper" the male with a fabric strip that is secured around his body to cover his penis. By placing a sanitary napkin inside this diaper, the urine can be absorbed instead dripping onto the floor or furniture. However, aim for complete house training and not for the remedy! Any dog that has continuing accidents or relapse after training should be checked for a bladder infection or stones.

There are products on the market that can serve as aids in house training, such as scented papers or sprays. Use those as directed but continue to follow the above schedule.

The hardest part of training a dog, is training the owner. An owner must teach his or her dog the rules and be consistent with them.

Last and most importantly, keep in mind that even the best trained dog will relapse from time to time. Don't expect perfection too soon, or you will stress yourself and your dog.

How to Kennel Train a Bichon Frise:

Kennel training is the most successful method of potty training a dog. This popular method involves keeping your Bichon Frise in a kennel while you can't provide supervision. This prevents it from eliminating in your home. Kennel training doesn't teach a dog to void in the kennel. Instead it deters the dog by forcing him to lie in his waste if he does eliminate. The ultimate goal of kennel training is to teach a dog to eliminate outside. Kennel training is typically the best method to train dogs that are difficult to housebreak, such as the Bichon Frise. While intelligent, Bichons aren't always cooperative with training methods, according to MyDogBreed.com. However, with patience, practice and persistence, you'll be able to successfully kennel-train your Bichon in a relatively short time.

Instructions:

1 – Provide your Bichon with the proper-sized kennel. The kennel should allow your Bichon room to stand up, turn around and lie down. Since Bichons are small, the kennel should be small. Allowing any more room will impede the training process since this method only works because it forces dogs to lie in their own waste if they eliminate. If the kennel is too big, the dog can simply walk away and kennel training will not be successful. Since every Bichon is different--some are small and some are large for their breed--there is no set size for the kennel. Take your Bichon with you to the store to see what will fit.

2 – Place the kennel where you want it in your home. Not only is the kennel a tool for housebreaking, it also serves as a doggie den. Place the kennel in an area that isn't busy. That way your Bichon can relax. When first introducing your Bichon to the kennel, place it close to you and leave the door open when you're around. Place treats and toys inside to entice your Bichon to enter and spend time inside. You want your Bichon to feel positive when inside.

3 – Establish a routine. Taking him out at the same times every day will help him learn how long he has to wait before relieving himself. For example, take your Bichon out as soon as you take him out of the kennel, before and after he sleeps and every few hours between. Soon, your Bichon will learn when he can go out. This will help him train his bladder and bowels.

4 – Give your Bichon his command every time you want him to void. Say this word when you take the Bichon out to his elimination area and be consistent with the word or phrase you use. In addition, use the same door and go to the same area every time you take him out to eliminate.

5 – Use rewards and praise when he voids in the appropriate area. Be sure the treat is small, since Bichons have tiny mouths and throats.

Aside from housetraining, there are other reasons to train your dog to use a kennel. By following the steps described here, success is assured. Once kennel trained, you'll assure that he'll be a happier and safer puppy.

Using a kennel is gentle and humane and dogs, being den animals, like their kennels because it is "home". The most important rule is consistency. Set up a schedule and stick with it for as long as it takes (and a week or two longer, just to be sure). The puppy is to be in his kennel at all times unless he is (a) out for a brief playtime or (b) being exercised. After he has urinated and/or had a bowel movement outside he can be let out to play for a brief period. Puppies like to eat and sleep so they really don't need to be out for long periods. They should always be kenneled at night and when you're away from home. This protects both the puppy and your furniture and carpets.

The key to training the puppy (or adult that has not been kenneled before) is to make going into the kennel a treat and not a punishment. Keep a container of puppy kibble nearby and each time the pup is put into his kennel, a single piece of kibble goes in first. He goes in to get his treat and the door is closed. Inside the kennel will be a small sized toy, one that cannot be swallowed or destroyed by chewing. If the pup fusses, speak to him and calm him. Once he is quiet, he can be removed from the kennel for cuddling – but never while he is being vocal. Not all pups can have a towel in the kennel, if they're chewers, but bedding also adds to the level of contentment.

It's important that there be playtime before putting him in the kennel so that he's tired and ready for a nap. Keeping the kennel near your chair is good because he feels your closeness and you can always stick a finger or two through the grate to let him lick and to reassure him that he's not alone. Once he stirs and is awake from his nap, take him outside, praise him to the hilt when he does his business and bring him in for a drink and more play-time.

Use a cheery voice for praise and a firm one for scolding - but Bichons do much better with praise than scolding! To scold him, pick him up and look him in the eye.

Anytime during the day when you can't give the puppy your full attention, he should be in his kennel. This means when you're on the phone, cooking, cleaning, dressing, playing, eating, sleeping, ad infinitum. If you're to be successful, you must watch him when he isn't kenneled. When you must leave the puppy longer and don't want to kennel him, use a small confined area free of dangerous electrical cords or anything that can be chewed. Leave his kennel with the door open for easy access.

Portable exercise pens can be purchased from dog supply vendors and are useful if you do not have a fenced yard. This is both a safety feature and a sanitary one. If your Bichon is a jumper or a digger, do not leave him unattended in either a yard or a fence. Electric fences are not good for Bichons, in part because it offers them no protection from stray dogs, dog-nappers or other unsafe conditions.

Bichons are bred to be companion animals and don't like being left at home alone for hours at a time. Consider this trait when buying your pet and make arrangements for someone to walk him when you're away.

Is kennel training important to the dog's health? First there is the safety issue. A lonely puppy looks for entertainment and that can be chewing electrical wires, children's toys, the drapes or furniture or anything small that is dropped on the floor. A kenneled puppy cannot reach these forbidden objects. A puppy in a home with children needs a safe and quiet retreat from overly affectionate children. The children should understand that when he goes into his house he is saying, "I'm tired and need to rest" and they should leave him alone.

A kennel can insure adequate rest. A puppy is still fragile and too much exercise can harm his young muscles and bones. A Bichon pup can have adequate exercise inside the house or brief supervised play-time outside in a restricted area. Bichons are fast runners and one can be in the street in the blink of an eye so leash training is also important.

Even adults can be fed in the kennel. This is to keep one pet from eating the other's food and the same theory would apply in a dog-cat household. An obese dog is unhealthy, as is one eating cat food on a regular basis. Even in a one animal home, the kennel should be his dining room because he eats quickly, rather than loitering over his meal. No one likes to have a picky eater. The water bowl sits nearby and is frequently washed and refilled because Bichons need fresh water available all the time.

Every dog has his day and some of those are sick days. Here is where his kennel is his comfort zone. It also means no accidents on the rug, if it is that kind of illness.   Postoperatively, the kennel becomes the recovery room.

Two of the biggest safety factors making it advisable to use a kennel are ones some pet owners never think of. A kenneled dog in an automobile has a much better chance of surviving an accident and a zero chance of causing an accident. He will also be welcome at hotels and in homes you visit if he is kenneled.

The dog that is kenneled when the family is away or during the night can be quickly picked up and moved away from danger in the event of a house fire, tornado or other tragic event. You don't have to know where to find him if he is always in the same location and that room should have a pet locator symbol on the window nearest his kennel. You should also let neighbors know where he will be, just as you would want them to know where to find your child in event of a fire.

These are just some of the ways that the kenneled dog has a better chance for a healthy, happy and safe life. As adults the kennel door can be left open and you will find that this is still a favorite retreat for naps or to escape the crowd. (Needless to say, no dog wants to be kenneled 24-7.) It is obvious to any owner of a kennel-trained dog that he does not feel it is his prison if the kennel is used properly. Now if we can only convince reluctant owners to understand that!

Barking:

Like most small dogs, the Bichon Frise is often too quick to sound the alarm at every new sight and sound. You have to be equally quick to stop your Bichon from turning into a barker. To do this successfully...

You must teach your Bichon to respect you. A dog who respects you will do what you say and will stop what he's doing when you tell him "No."

If your Bichon barks obsessively, you can cure this behavior. It's important to teach your dog to speak but it's just as important to teach him NOT to bark. If your dog barks when the doorbell rings and this is permissible behavior, mark the bark by rewarding your dog with a treat and also with a command such as "good." Once your Bichon perfects the desired behavior you can add the command "speak" just before he barks. Be sure not to reward your dog until you give the verbal cue. Your dog will quickly learn that he only gets a treat if he performs the desired behavior.

Now it is time to add the command "quiet" or "no bark." When your dog is quiet you can reward him with a treat and the verbal command that you have chosen. Your dog will quickly learn that unless you give the command "speak" he should be quiet.

Dog barking can be an annoying and difficult habit to break in your Bichon Frise dog. Because of how high-pitched their bark can be, it can often cause headaches and annoy your neighbors. On top of this, there is no direct way to tell your dog to stop barking because it will not understand you. Bichon Frise dogs are infamous for their tendency to bark in short yelps. However, you can do something to stop this annoying bark.

1 – Get several small-sized treats that you can have access to easily if your Bichon Frise starts barking. These should be small, bite-sized treats that the dog can smell easily. A strong, bacon-scented treat will work the best.

2 – Wait for your dog to start barking. When it does start barking, present it with one of the treats and issue a command like "stop barking." Since the Bichon Frise cannot bark and sniff simultaneously, it will instinctively stop barking to sniff the treat. However, doing this once will not be enough to break the dog's habit entirely.

3 – Continue doing this for several days to several weeks. Bichon Frise dogs are some of the most vocal with their barking, so it may take longer than this. However, eventually, they will learn the command to stop barking and will do so without a treat reward. Do not get frustrated with the dog. Outrage or violence can set it back in its training. Be calm when offering the treat, and praise it when it stops barking.

According to the breed standard, Bichon Frises should be gentle mannered, sensitive, playful and affectionate. But since they love human company, they tend to demand much attention. This may result in whining, too much howling and barking. A howling or barking small dog can be considered tolerable in broad daylight but if the barking takes place when everyone is asleep, then it's another story. It can be distracting not only to you but to your neighbors as well.

First, find out the reason for whining or barking. Is he barking near the door? If so, perhaps he needs to go potty or there is someone or something outside the door. If his bark from the kitchen can be heard upstairs, it's more likely he's terrified of being alone or he's not comfortable in his current setting. If you have uncovered the reason, address the issue and provide the things that would suit him best. He may need a blanket to keep him warm during cold days or he may need to transfer to a cooler area when its summer. If it's his first night in your home, you may want to let him sleep inside your room or in any area where he can see you. Then gradually increase the distance between the two of you until he gets used to sleeping in the area you want.

When it comes to toilet breaks, know that puppies can't control their bladder so you have to take them out every hour until they have established their potty schedule. Also, it helps to watch out for signs that your pet needs to go and make sure to take him out to potty before going to bed to keep your dog from barking.

If your dog barks or whines because of separation anxiety, there are Bichon Frise training methods that can help you address the issue. The training doesn't need to be harsh or complicated, just a few sessions on getting your dog used to being alone and you leaving the house. Additionally, you also have to make it clear to your dog that whining, howling or barking is unacceptable by ignoring him each time he barks and rewarding him if he's quiet.

Behavior good and bad

One of the most desirable qualities in a Bichon is its beautiful temperament. "A cheerful attitude is the hallmark of the breed and one should settle for nothing less." The show breeder expects from birth for each pup to have the potential to be a big winner in the ring and works from the beginning to enhance the basic sound temperament bred into the pup. The pups are handled gently, kept warm, fed well and socialized beginning at a very young age. Unfortunately, pups bred for profit may not have this kind of care because it takes time and effort to give this special attention.

Even with the best of care, some pups will have "soft" temperaments and may not have the enthusiastic attitude to make a good show prospect. This is one of the reasons for placing some beautiful Bichon pups in pet homes instead of show homes. Lucky is the new owner who has gotten one of these lovable and playful puppies! They still make exceptional pets and have had the advantage of good early care by the breeder.

Why do some pups then become biters or seem to become very shy? Why do some pet-shop Bichons turn into wonderful outgoing adults? What makes the difference? Obviously good temperament genes will overcome even careless handling. Unfortunately, even good genes will not tolerate bad handling and well-mannered Bichons can become biters or become aggressive in other ways.

It is important to understand that there are degrees of shyness that can lead to various types of temperament problems. The mildly shy Bichon will not do well in the show ring but becomes a delightful pet. The very shy dog can become quite aggressive, to the point of biting, unless properly handled. This is called "fear aggression" and these dogs may also suffer "separation anxiety", a totally different temperament problem.

To avoid fear aggression, the pup needs training in a puppy kindergarten class (a type of obedience training for puppies). This should be a class that uses positive reinforcement training methods. The basis for this training is that the pup is praised, possibly given a small treat and given positive attention for good behavior and punishment is never a part of the training. Pups benefit from socialization, which is simply exposing the puppy to many types of situations in a positive way. Read the article *CREATING A PUPPY YOU CAN LIVE WITH* for more information.

Suppose your puppy is already biting your hand or nipping at your clothes. This kind of behavior is not to be tolerated. A firm "NO" is called for and sometimes it helps to take the pup's muzzle in your hand and to give the head a gentle shake while saying "NO". Now do something to distract the puppy, such as giving him a toy to play with. Once the pup has behaved in a more desirable way, you can tell him what a "Good boy" he is. Never pick the pup up and cuddle him while he is behaving badly. This only says to him that his behavior is desirable and gets him attention – not a lesson that you're trying to teach. Some of this biting behavior may come from painful teething but you still must not tolerate it.

If your puppy has been well-behaved and starts to show signs of biting or other aggressive behavior, you must examine the way you're playing with the puppy (or that your children are playing with him). Teasing is the biggest cause of developing bad temperament. Roughhouse play; taking toys away as the pup is reaching for them or while he is playing; tug of war games; these are all examples of bad play habits that can have disastrous results. A puppy should never be disturbed while he is eating. In other words, look at what is happening in the puppy's life that has created an angry puppy when he should have a "cheerful attitude", as described in the Bichon standard.

If your pup has developed aggressive habits and you're not able to solve them, get him into an obedience class that uses positive reinforcement so he can learn better behavior and you can learn how to handle him better!

Separation anxiety is the name of the problem that occurs when your dog absolutely can**not** tolerate having no one at home with him. Any Bichon should be able to be alone for a few hours at a time, though many don't handle being alone all day long. The Bichon is bred to be a companion animal; expecting him to live alone doesn't take into account this innate part of his nature.

The dog with true separation anxiety won't want to be alone for minutes, to say nothing of tolerating hours alone. This is the dog that needs special handling and possibly medication. Begin by training him to accept your absence for 2 minutes, then 5 minutes and work up to being away for ½ hour or an hour at a time. Give him something to play with and step outside the door for just seconds, working it up to longer periods of time each day. This is actually specialized conditioning and may best be done with the help of a trained obedience handler or behavioral expert. For the dog with true separation anxiety, discuss with your veterinarian whether he needs medication to improve his ability to handle your absence. The medication should be a part of a package that combines retraining along with the medication and should not be relied upon to be effective without proper conditioning (training).

Remember that it's the nature of this breed to be a wonderful and loving companion to his family and his basic instinct is to be your very best friend. If he's not acting in such a loving and trusting way, there's probably a good reason for it. Play detective and determine what has happened to him to change him from the sweet tempered little guy that he should be. Time and a little effort will help you both to rediscover that affectionate little puppy that every Bichon should be!

Author's Last Words

Thank you for reading my book. If you truly enjoyed it, would you kindly leave a non-biased review on Amazon or Goodreads.com? Thank you again and I hope you will review our other books and recommend our products to your family and friends. Please feel free to ask questions or comment at my author page at: www.amazon.com/author/john_williams.

With Gratefulness,
–John Williams

Author Resources

Bichon Frise Unique Among Dogs – Kindle Edition

Bichon Frise Unique Among Dogs – Paperback Edition

Bichon Frise parmi les chiens – Kindle French Edition

Bichon Frise parmi les chiens – Paperback French Edition

Bichon Frise Unique Among Dogs – Chinese Edition (Digital Download)

Pomeranian Breed Of A Queen – Kindle Edition

Pomeranian Breed Of A Queen – Paperback Edition

The Boxer Scholar And Clown – Kindle Edition

The Boxer Scholar And Clown – Paperback Edition

German Shepherd: Loyal, Powerful & Noble – Kindle Edition

German Shepherd: Loyal, Powerful & Noble – Paperback Edition

Take Charge Of Your Aviation Career – Kindle Edition

Take Charge Of Your Aviation Career – Paperback Edition

Associated Apps
Bichon Frise App
iTunes Store Link (Apple)

Bichon Frise App Google Play (Android)